Guest Host

Guest Host

elizabeth hughey

The National Poetry Review Press
Aptos, California

The National Poetry Review Press
(an imprint of DHP)
Post Office Box 2080, Aptos, California 95001-2080

Printed in the United States of America
Published in 2012 by The National Poetry Review Press

ISBN 978-1-935716-20-4

Cover artwork:

Twos
by David Konigsberg,
collection of Charlene and Keith Goggin

davidkonigsberg.us

For Jan

TABLE OF CONTENTS

Etiquettes

we are saying thank you faster and faster
with nobody listening we are saying thank you
thank you we are saying and waving
dark though it is

W.S. Merwin

Whose doorstep are we standing on
        anyway with its climbing ivy and brass
lion knocker? The way one door sometimes

opens all of them, we become the same.
        My fridge is your fridge. My cleaver
is yours. When you leave, you leave

a part of you here, and that part of me
        that never leaves tends to what is left
of you. They have the kind of time

we could never have, dipping fingers
        into jams, while you and I are off
to the next garden party, our perfumes trailing

behind us like loyal hounds. Gold beads
        loosen and skip on the stone
patio, tiny fists pounding on doors.

Do not think there is less of you to leave.
        We can make more of ourselves. Not
new selves, but old ones, not improving,

but returning, cleaner, more naked,
        dropping leaves like winter trees to see
more sky, more city lights. You in your home

and me in mine, wrapped in our terry cloths,

we look at the same blinking tower, or we
are looking at the same blinking light,

or we are looking for the darkness
          between the blinks, knowing that
the dark is what we share over the acreage.

WAXING OR WANING, WE DIDN'T KNOW

We were stirring pitchers of juleps. The hummingbirds were sparring. Poverty dawned on us. I said if hummingbirds were as big as poverties, we'd all be sipped through the beaks of plantation owners who loll on their porches in the closed books of historical libraries. Have you seen how that trembling bullet pauses to swallow? Aren't we all sugar and water, mostly. I heard the hunger of hummingbirds swooping for our pocketbooks. I felt preyed upon in the nicest way, like it's either that flicker of a bird or me that's going to drop out of a sky that I don't even know I'm flying in.

THE TREATMENT OF WINDOWS

They were flung open, they were shattered by rocks, they were sat upon and sung out of and climbed through. Some were painted shut. Some were barred. Some were tinted. Most were metaphors. We stood at a window open to a heath and became watercolor images of ourselves. From skyscrapers, we watched an airplane crawl across the sky and felt like the undercast of clouds beneath it. When our girlfriends failed us, we said our window faced a brick wall. We complained of windowless cubicles and refused to call our monitors and televisions what they were. When we finally fell in love, we felt our window opening into another and we climbed from one to the other, the whistle of traffic beneath us. We were pulled onto soft carpet and stood to see our old window already occupied by another lonely stargazer. Then, we got confused. A window is an opening that makes it possible to see something. A tree is a window to the earth it grows in. The night sky opens into the deep well within us. Coins are falling, falling. We saw our lives for what they were, windows, but who was looking? We felt blackened. We felt camouflaged. We were black bears ambling in the night forest. We grew to love the soft outlines of our frames. Then, those, too, disappeared, and we, too, with them.

MING DYNASTY CHAIR

It feels like I'm sitting on a conversation between
rosewood and veneer. I wish that I were looking in
on us and not sitting across from you. I wish I felt

you looking in on me while I loop my spoon
through the bisque. We can learn from this china
pattern. See how we could be reclining under

an etched magnolia? We could be those sterling
raindrops wobbling on a branch. Quivering
can be much better than flowering. What is this

fork in my hand? Is it Waverly? Is it Fleury?
This pattern is repetitive, like we are not dining,
but driving, down the same twisting road

in different cars. No, we are reaching out
for the same wire of prayer and hope
we've grabbed it, that it's not some invisible

insect we believe we've caught in our palms.
In our right hands, we hold our blades.
We are joining forces. We are at war,

the old kind of war, organized and decorated
with furs and colored flags. We line up our soldiers
and blow a horn to begin. Don't ask

what we are fighting for. It is not for us to know.

Just keep your napkin in your lap, unless of course,
you must excuse yourself. Then, lay the napkin

on your chair, unless of course, you are finished
with the war, then leave the napkin next to your
plate. Only then will it be safe to explode into bloom.

The guests are billeted to their quarters, the men striking matches and the women coughing into hankies. Hear the drone of electric razors and feel the explosive thunder from the neighboring screen. Laugh, now. Laugh, again. Watch the bachelor toss on the couch splashed with jungle flowers. Howl. You are a hound called to the hearth. You want in. Scratch at the door, smelling a hen wrapped and tied in the icebox of your memory, a memory before you were born, in your bones, an instinct. You are a well-bred blur, a shadow on the stoop. On the other side of the screen is a life that is part yours. You own it like an escalator or an airport terminal. A public life. And how many you have lived in a day, in a year, loving common women into higher classes, massaging your mustache, jotting facts into your notebooks. What do they really say? Scribbledy scribble. The encyclopedias are painted wood. The vodka bottle is filled with water. Still, you drink it. Shot glass by shot glass, you gulp it down. You are getting thirstier and more sober. The usher helps you out of your seat. You drive slowly in case someone is following you. At home, you undress quickly and crawl into bed. You pretend to sleep, sure that you are still being watched. You can hear an audience clapping from your neighbor's apartment. They'll clap for you next.

RUE SAINT CLAUDE

Don't be sad for the actress weeping for her son on Rue Saint Claude. There are enough theatergoers sobbing for her. Be sad for the street, Rue Saint Claude, that doesn't exist. If Rue Saint Claude is not there, then the boy on his back on the sidewalk on Rue Saint Claude isn't there. One day, he will wake up and be only a small piece of himself, the size of the pendant swinging from his neck. Look there, at the gold, and your reflection in the gold. That is your small self, the part of you that will get up out of your velvet chair, wounds and all, and walk down Rue Saint Claude, down down into the hole that is your home now, and you will let the top lid touch the bottom lid. Then, you will have many mothers.

THE SMALL BIRD THAT FOLLOWS THE HAWK

I was sitting cross-legged
in the park, meditating
in a dream. I heard a man
uncross his legs
in a passing train.
I was reading
in my daydream.
It was a novel
about sleep. I heard a man
put his ear to the ground.
He was listening
for us to cross his front yard.
We were in the backyard
setting up our tent.
This is where I dreamed
I was sleeping in a hotel.
A man had a voice
like a stone corridor.
I listened for sock feet.
In a dream I stood
at the hotel window.
Has this happened
to you? The ocean
shining through the glass
colored the whole room —
the drapes, loveseat,
bedspread, lampshades —
blue. I said, *It is just*
as though I were awake.

Your ticket is for entering a new unimportance
that insists it is all made of glass, smooth enough
to be skied upon, connecting what is above
the water to what is below. You are connected
to the Midwest because your river is connected,
but you are made of non-river elements, too.
You can see how the river is also the skier
and the mother of the skier, who was born
in Omaha, and without Omaha, we wouldn't
have the mother, and without grain, we wouldn't
have the mother, and without the sun, gilding.

So you see the sun in the water, but sun already
plays a role in tidal water. What is not river,
anyway? Sometimes a river is said to be larger
than a creek, but this is not always true. Some rivers
flow as several interconnecting streams of water,
a braided river. The occasional interstate blackout
in the Northeast illuminates: when a single line fails
and we all fail, the result is a new wakefulness
that is very old, starting with sounds, birds,
hush of the road, and the people on the road,
and how those who woke before help us to wake.

Never speak of it. Be silent as the little b in *debt*.
Just lean into the graceful pull of the downward spiral.
You have a lovely field of numbers. How they blossom
and thrive when you are away.
Be clothed in the petals of the nothing that you have.
A hole is useful only through its emptiness.
Plant your emptiness. Like a potted fern on a train, you
will be pulled by sunlight out of a speeding window
                            and unfurl your green palms.

I can't see the night
because the night
doesn't want me in it.
Go inside, says the night,
but I can't make myself
vanish from someone else's
mind. Arms out, slaps
of cold leaves, I find the knob
and go in. Your mind
is a dark classroom,
and I am a slide projected
on the cinder blocks.
When you type me
into another scene,
I feel reborn, but
the feeling passes
and I feel only 35.
I probably want to
fall in love. Maybe
I have a heart condition.
No, I am running
to answer the telephone.
No, I am the voice
on the telephone calling
with terrible news.
I am the terrible news.
I want to be a gate
swung open. I will be
one barb in a wire,

and you can zoom
away from me until
I blend into the pasture.

Write this down: A man kisses a man with a song in his face.
Two: The lullaby must be pulled from the throat
like a rooted fern. Three: The goat path crosses the spring.
Four: Floating masses of gulfweed. Five: The quick, agile
skid steer replaced the pitchfork. Six: A man hugs a man
to pass this on: *If a man's fingers are indelibly stained,*
he would better wear white gloves. Seven: The shavings
of a city pile up on the shores. Eight: Notes, as though
carbonated, rise up through the floorboards. Nine:
In his telephone voice, a man prays to a man.
Ten: Please, lighten this planet I carry in my flatbed.

ON ENDING A LETTER

A moth in your ear
like carved words
under white paint
on a bench in a garden
of Berlin.
I am gone.
I can be made again
with slippers on hardwood.
A footstep lifts off the floor
and flutters through the wall.
Gone again, yet I remain
very truly yours.

WHEN TO SNOWBALL

You left us there, in our kitchens, untying our aprons.
You left us in our bedrooms, spanking the pillows. You
left us in department stores applying our lipsticks in
Zinzolin and Bellini. You left us in restrooms clasping
our pocketbooks, tipping the girls. You left us frozen
in our rabbit earmuffs on the slopes of Gatlinburg. We
opened our Avocado freezers, and you left us, and we
never closed a door again. We can't pick up the receiver.
We can't steam the drapes. We cannot remove the
flaming rump from the oven. We are sitting on our sofas
in Bisque and Brulet, and we are opening our magazines.
We are in the magazines. We are reproduced. There you
will find us, in *Vogue* and in *Sister*. You can rip us out. You
can smell our inky bodies. You can ask for our hairstyles
at the salon. You can bake our cherry fools. You can
cover our wingbacks in Pavement and Portobello. Set
our jewels in your pendants. You will try us on. You will
think you feel like us. You will feel new and improved.
Smoking without the smoke. You are clouding up,
though. You are discoloring. You are becoming a little
less born every day. And we are preserved. We are
glistening in our gelatins in darkened refrigerators. If we
are in the dark, though, then, you are in the dark. We
can't help but contain you. Recall our photograph. Was it
the flash, or were we closing our eyes to see you better?

Lying in your bed after watching your short film in which children leap into flight, I know that I have been used. I have always felt like the muse of car commercials and stenciled billboards. I've always felt like I could be the shape of somebody's pancake. I should be waking up now. I should be breathing breath into your mouth. Did the ground shake, or just the things on the ground – houses, armoires? Today, I will be the white radish that stays plugged into its earth. I have had enough light. I have been captured in enough photographs. Now, I will wait for something to look at. I will wait for someone to bring me my eyes. Here are yours. And here are your keys.

It is a morning after.
It is a next day
and I am godly
standing in my doorway
looking down at the water,
which is held down
by the mist.
Then the clouds
are dragged away
in tiny pieces
like sugar mounds
by insects. The dumb
blue sky, the clear
dumb lake.
Trilling begins,
but the birds aren't
telling us a thing.
I feel smarter
than the stick pines
for knowing at least
something, that yesterday,
the boy was pulled out of
the water, and then stood
on his pale, fat legs and cried.

I am thinking of bridges
and how the view
doesn't try, the mountains
roll over like caged lions,

the sails in the bay, sharp claws
ripping the air. I'm thinking
of what I know and now
it seems like not much,
but still more than the stupid
sand with orphan roots.

I like it in movies
when soldiers run
through rose gardens
and crash into tables
of sherry glasses,
boots clomping mud
through marble hallways.
I like when bombs shatter
stained glass windows
while a man covers
a woman under the raining
shards, in movies. And when
the quarterback falls
out of bounds, knocking
over the camera man,
and the two must be pulled
from their embrace.

I have not yet been pulled
from an embrace
but I have felt the love
of gravity on my back,
like the sun that I am
turning away from
turning back indoors
toward a blue screen

where the ending
is known, at least by
someone, a group
of men and women
in office chairs around
a black oval table,
craning necks to see
the white board
with three possible
endings. Narrowed
down to two, then one:
The driver swerves
the boat into a soft,
sandy bank.

It's a comedy, now.
The wedding party
is thrown overboard in
suits and silks. A groom
dumps a trout
out of his top hat.
The captain wrings
out his notes. The couple
kisses, ankle-deep in water.
I am not thinking about
the couple, though. I am
thinking about the fish
pulsing his gills at the bottom
of the studio pool, chased
and lifted by the green
net and dropped back
into the familiar waters
of his tank, and the tank

covered and secured
in the back of the handler's
van, driving west toward
a garage apartment on the coast,
sloshing and bumping the edges
of the glass with his blushing,
bright mottled body.

II.

Shaking Hands

A PRIVATE DWELLING

Soap bubbles, the ornaments
of a morning, float in the wait.

Somewhere in the Atlantic,
a tropical storm becomes

a hurricane, as I am looking out
the window for the plumber.

Nothing pops. The blinds grid
the mirror of tea in the cup.

Behind every mirror is a depth
of water, and things from this side

keep falling in. The tinkling
of spoons. The whispers of

appliances. Facets of jewels.
I'm putting on my face

at the dressing table, as if bracing
for the winds. Here he comes.

No, here he comes. He is seeing
himself in my window, and his tools

are splashing, slipping from his belt.
Now, the plumber is waiting for me.

The door will be opened. Mud will be
tracked in. The bathtub will stop

its welling. The trundle of the house
will shake the cups in their saucers.

We will move on, graphed as we are
in the varnished reception of our vocations.

It's not about the woman, it's about what's all around her.
Acanthine drapes with narrow leaves, their pointed lobes
conjoined with a spine. Two chairs with their suggestions
not to sit. The scrolling growth of creases her hip makes
on the bedspread. Not how she looks, but how you feel
when you see her. You are pulled free from the branch
by her smoky winds. And how she divides herself
from the other leaves who flit the through the air.
Here they are, she says. *All your little tonights,*

and not a tomorrow among them.

Front doors open
in time for the first
globes of daylight
to land upon the lawn.
A tennis ball
has a destiny
before it leaves
the window.
A man dressed
like a newspaper
lands on the doorstep.
The baby grand lifts
a curtain of song
through the treetops.
A pedal
is a foot-operated lever.
A petal
is the showy part
of a flower. Petalous
means having petals.
So does petaliferous.

YOU, A BARELY

Began the way a leaf
could have been a petal,
the way the song
keeps starting over,
you keep beginning,
you've been being born
for a long time, but I
don't know when
you began, the way a hand
could have been a hip,
and a pelvis a bowl
and a bowl a jar
of river water, unshaken.
The way the silt settles,
but I'm not looking
at the silt, I'm looking
through the water
to see you, a faint,
shivering ray. The way
a sun could have already
faded, when we are still
lit up, we are aflame.
Burn the whole forest
and another reappears.

Helen felt like a garment, which had, through constant handling, become faded and rumpled. She was on a very crowded train in which there was promiscuous shoving. After leaving the subway and asking a few strangers, Helen found a dormitory. She took an elevator up to a quiet floor. There, she found an unlocked door that opened into a dim room. She fondled her way to a sofa. Helen slept and woke early, exiting unnoticed in the blue haze of dawn. How to get back? A friend had left phone messages in the night. *Meet us back at the apartment. Bring more ice.* But what is the address? She thought of the guys rolling over to wrap their arms around soft women. She missed the one she might have slept with. Standing on the quad, she found herself turning toward strangers. The morning was getting colder, and her wool coat had turned thin. To Helen, taking the bicycle felt like stealing a wheelchair, but it was all coming back to her as her feet started to pedal.

The Wright brothers had a sister. When she flew in the machine called a "fixed-wing aircraft," she tied rope around her shins to keep her skirt down. Why is this important? Because I am going to write a dissertation on it. I will look at the world through a chandelier tied up with mosquito netting. The sad thing about a bore is that she thinks that everything is so interesting. I'm here to tell you that it's not. My office smells like a camera shop. I know a furniture store that smells like a bakery, and a bakery that smells like a clean baby, and a baby that smells like the soap it was carved out of. Take her home. Bathe with her. She is not disappearing. She is dissolving. Step out of the bath without rinsing. Do not rinse her off your skin. You can never rinse her off. She is your sister, too. Her name is Katherine Wright.

You know how it feels to be driving back to the party
rental store with stacks of lowballs clicking in their
crates, because you are driving back to the party rental
store with stacks of lowballs clicking in their crates. You
are the fat jockey weighing down the horse, pulling left
like a stuck wheel on a shopping cart. How could you
come into this world without a wallet? How could you
arrive into your body without a bone? And yet, here
you are, climbing a tree on the radio to retrieve a shoe
thrown by bullies. Last night, in the near dark of the
fireplace, you looked down into your glass and felt the
breath of the stallion. Every painting on the wall seemed
to depict a race, but maybe you were just taught that
every still life contains a conflict at its core, and you see
the battle between orange and pear, and what makes
you the maddest has no color, no muscle, no material to
slash. So, the knife is missing. So what. So is the fucking
cocktail shaker. And you are going to have to pay for
that shit.

That day at the tracks, the men outran the horses.
I saw a fashion designer tell a policeman what to do.
I saw ladies looking at other ladies in compact
mirrors. Stallions kicked up clouds of face powder.
Why? Because the day was designed by a famous man
and assembled by construction workers who shower
after work. A tweed suit shook a doorknob like hand.
A door mistook a woman for a wall. A woman opened
her blouse in front of a window. She pretended nobody
was looking.   Nobody was looking.

I'm carrying a baby inside a belly inside a floral blouse that serves as a dress. I'm looking at a television through a shop window through which, by reflection, I see a floral blouse. Cantering horses hover at my throat. To go on, to leave, will mean missing my cue. I stay still and listen. Three boys pass on bikes spitting out cusswords. Is that it? A car door. Is that it? Then another. Wait for it. The siren. Wait for it. The church bell. Then, I hear it, inside my chest, like an animal turning beneath the porch. I clutch my purse. I smooth my ponytail. I step through the doors saying, "Oh, I am so very sorry for your loss."

It is like my face is fixed in one
expression, like the window
is stuck looking out into one
day. The red truck passes. At 3 a.m.,
I get up and do all the work.
The dishes, the clothes, the garbage.
In the morning, I wake into the same 7
where nothing has been done. The red
truck drives by. What do you call
this kind of rain? That you can't
actually see. Not even the lights
turned off. Or, the mail opened.

Is this car I'm in a Saturn?
It makes me want to orbit something.
I think we are being orbited by that bird.
What could that train be carrying at this time of day?
Probably something emotional, like baseball cards
and cassette tapes – things we keep in our attic.

It's so tempting to get out of this car. I feel like
I have mail. I feel like there's a department store
that just got a shipment of pewter finches.
And also bags of colored feathers. And Mylar balloons!
Recordings of our voices when we were children.
Greeting cards with real handwriting, saying things like,
There is nothing you could ever do to keep me
from loving you, and, Happy Month-iversary!
and, I'm sorry if I hurt your feelings.

I'm sorry if I hurt your foot. No, I'm sorry
if you think your foot is hurt, and I'm sorry
that you think I hurt it. I was just driving around
town looking for a Kentucky Derby party.
I don't even think I saw you in the parking lot.
I wish I were hungrier, but I also wish I were a tiger.

A CENTERPIECE

How those hydrangeas
stay dead upon the bush
through the winter.
That's the perfect nude
for lips and lighting.
I need the yellow
of a whiffle ball bat
left out in the rains.
Pull the outside in
and toss it over
your coffee table.
That's sea grass.
That's hay. Live in it.
Live in it more.
A wallpaper forest
of birches; they make
a something where
a nothing used to be.
That is the way babies
happen. That is the way
convicts get paroled.
I want the blue
between the clouds
when you are focused
on the clouds.
That's azure. No, Azure
is a high school girl trying
to say something. That's me
trying to say something.

Listen for the unjailing
of periwinkle, of seafoam.
Now you aren't saying a thing.

1.

Will a boy wake in the night and hear his way out of a room into a dark hall, past a painting of a pear too dim to see? When he hears his feet on the carpet, will there be carpet? What about sleet tapping the window? Will his ears create the snowplow shaking snow from a bush? I just want to know if a sound can create a boy. Or, if a woman becomes a mother when she thinks she hears a baby crying for her.

2.

What should I get for the woman who is disappearing?
I want to stop saying "I," but I don't know any other
way to say it. How many horses do you hear right now?
Is there another way to say that the grasses are choking
the winter? When I stand in the desert, the vastness gets
inside me the way the ocean gets inside the marble. I
feel dimmed down. I feel smudged with eraser marks.
What am I?

3.

Did you go to the show? Did you clap when everyone clapped? Did you stand very still and let the crowd move your shoulders? Was there a girl way down front who never turned around? Do you remember when standing behind a girl with your arms around her waist had never happened to you before? Was that before you knew about the word *juxtaposition*? Was that when you played the saxophone? Do you think you can really know someone by the swing of her ponytail? Do you ever write letters to yourself as a boy? Now that you think about it, as a boy, did you ever feel like someone was trying to send you a letter? Was it about Lenny? Was it about the sax?

4.

Am I useful? Am I entirely suitable for the position I occupy? If I were eliminated, would I be missed? Would someone else look better in my place? Or would my place look better empty? One drop joins the ocean, but the ocean doesn't become more of anything or less. Should I join the ocean? Should I just join the sea?

5.

What is the best way to ask a question? What alone is impolite. We say *pardon*. Say *mam*. The British say *sorry*. *What* is the glowworm jarred and dimming. *What* is the column of breath blown into the changing of the season. What about the sound of a thimble dropped into a bucket of paint? What is left when the last curtsy changes from a liquid to a vapor? The dew we carry on our skins.

6.

Emily, I have a question, but it isn't for you. It isn't for
anybody. If it were a gift, I would forget to give it to you.
It's not even for me to ask. I received an answer today in
the form of a question, and I have accidentally answered
it myself.

AFTER A WILLIAM JAMES QUOTE
ABOUT THE OCEAN

It might have been the fish, the shellfish, the – what is that called – octopus – what do you call that – calamari – the whole baby octopus seeped in red broth that made me think of the sea and how far away from it I really was, a day's drive, a whole day without stopping for caffeine, for candy that rips the tentacles off your tongue. That I was far from the sea made me feel far away from love. I was far away from a wool blanket under which we would watch for whales, but then again, when did the whales ever come? We watched from that cliff with its suicidal ghosts, its ladies in silks crackling on the rocks, and the tourists, red in the face, too much sour wine and baskets of bread. But the whales, when they did come, came up like a storm of seagulls reflected in the water. I am lying about the whales. You would know if you had ever seen one, the quiet flip of a tail, spit of water. And this whale is above your head. It is the sea-dark shadow drawn across your face, which I am sitting across from so far from the sea.

In the tub, I read an article on water called "The Last Drop" by Michael Specter. I wonder if Michael Specter is in his pool house reading my poem about a pool house. In it, I say that peeing outdoors before a wedding while the girls are watching the bride get her hair done is like knowing that a crooked river burst into flames in 1969. Yesterday, I didn't know that. Nor did I know that it takes more than a thousand drops of water to make one drop of coffee. I tell you this because I am writing an article about water called "The Last Drop." When I drink coffee again, I will think about all the drops of water that went into making my coffee. I wonder how many drops of coffee it takes to make one drop of bathwater. I will add "water consumption" to my list of items to consider at bedtime. After that, I will drift off to sleep wondering if anyone is thinking of me as she drifts off to sleep.

INVITATION BY PHONE

Is that you, Sarah? Are you free for dinner? Oh, that's too bad. Is it the war? On what channel? Yes, I see the nursing mothers gathering in the shade. No, I don't know how you could be free for dinner when there is so much suffering on the television. It's 120 degrees in Chad and also at Lake Havasu. They are connected by their climates. There is a word for that: *Isotherm*. You know what sounds beautiful if you don't know what it means? *Alopecia*. And, *Nocturia*. No, you're right, we shouldn't enjoy such loveliness when other people are in pain. I just keep finding more things beautiful, even the aqua blue detergent I'm pouring into the basin. And the residue of whiskers circling the drain. What if we enjoy less when all the wars are over? I am going to miss geraniums. I'd like to go back to 1945 just to celebrate the end of a war. Please come drink pink champagne with me! We can set off fireworks in my cellar.

Any coastal town might take you in
after a long drive from Detroit.
Any bus may sigh to a stop and unfold its doors.
There are rest stops, though, with rows of vending
machines: ones for lattes, ones for hard candies,
ones for disposable toiletries (razors, swabs).

Dear travelers with your coins digested by the whirring,
punch the number for what you need.
You may get an extra
if you are open to revelations wrapped in cellophane.
Trainer planes sharpen their aerial combat skills above
while I practice softening my vision on the windshield.

Pensacola has been in my employ as a lover
for thirty six years.
Expansive in sky, picnic-able, easily painted,
Pensacola is leaving,
to my regret, because I am closing one of my eyes.

If you are ready to love Pensacola, then refold
this letter and return it to the envelope marked, "Yes."

III.

Oaxaca

Flower   flower   flower   flower
Today for the sake of all the dead. Burst into flower.

Muriel Rukeyser

Oaxaca the dawn was a film of the dawn.
Oaxaca I stood in the shower and thought of Bulgaria.
Oaxaca Bulgaria. Oaxaca the hotel.
Oaxaca we had a better song for birthdays.
Oaxaca a man would come to every home
in which a man was dying, that a president
would come, like a nurse into a house of the dying,
into this country and help not just the dying
but those of us who are still very young.
And we were better at dying, of course,
not at dying, but at convalescing.

Oaxaca your dad wasn't dying.
Oaxaca your corduroy pants were easier to spell,
and you weren't shrinking inside them.
Oaxaca nobody said "at least."
Oaxaca the crane in that song was a wild boar,
and that song was written down
and played for infants to help them wake.

Wake up Oaxaca you can.
Let me put on your shoes.
Let me pull back your hair.
Oaxaca there were something that would arrive
in the mail, that you could go to the post office today
or turn on the television and there it would be,
Sofia, the city! A city for sick fathers where you could
drink wine with your breath, where breathing was
drinking, and you were so hungry, and here come

the trays of gleaming meats, thick soups,
bread for sopping. Oaxaca you could be so full.

A door grows so wide it swallows the building it was meant to open. I am meant to open. I open so much that I engulf myself and disappear. I can't find Oaxaca, but I know exactly where it is. In Julie's memory. How walking on the sand with Jason felt like stealing someone's hot shower. How Oaxaca seemed painted over a Mayan city. Oaxaca, that textbook of murders. Death May Die, say the t-shirts. Long Live Death, say the billboards. The Gulf of California is the answer. The question: Where was Oaxaca when the great bridge of knowledge buckled and all the piano keys turned black?

When I step back from your globe,
I see no Mexico. The Americas
flounder like a t-shirt on the bottom
of a pool. At first, I am heartbroken
when I return to the place I thought
you'd be. I thought you were many
you's, but you are just one you.
And you must think I am more
than one Liz. I thought we had
more seasons. I thought if I didn't like
the weather, I could wait a minute.
A minute is up, and you are still
mostly cloudy. A bonfire still embers
                    under your sands.

Just get in.
Get in and blow up.
A t-shirt inflated
with breath.
A callisthenic
misspelling
of *tomorrow*,
of *Oaxaca*.
Silversmiths,
please wake up
again and polish us
a new anthem,
evoke the smoothness
of the insides
of seashells, share
adjectives such as
crepuscular with the late
morning sun's italic
something on the water.

Because a shadow is light crossed out, cross out the gray bird. Cross out the couple on the beach walking like a W holding hands. Walk like L, lovers. Walk like an X, crossing out the hurting, the lost, the beggars of the world. Insert the lifeguards, the ambulance drivers. Where it says *collapse of schools, hospitals, and factories*, put *the birthplace of hot springs*. Where it says *bleeding*, write in *sailing*, as in, *She noticed she was sailing*. Where it says, *corpse*, write, *dense herbage and foliage*. Lovers: steal boats and bleed toward the shared darks of gun barrels and mouths.

FOR THE VOICEOVER

I was looking it up:
the word for a sharp turnaround in the polls.
Where is that sharp turn in mood on the map,
and how can August be so October?
How can Ottawa be so Oaxacan?
Not by temperature but by the taste of the tap water.
Of pennies. Of quarries.
I am looking it up. How do you say *help*
with your hands?
A hand-drawn hand signing O. A. X. A. C. A.
Spell *Bougainvillea*. Spell *Oscilloscope*.
Spell *airplane* and hop on the back of my hand.

1.
Cousin, if you cry, a soft hand
plays a hard song on the playa.
Why sob for a woman you hardly know?
By woman, I mean samba. And by
hardly know, I mean the drugstore in Tijuana
that you drove past on the way.

2.
In Oaxaca, a fruit falls from a branch.
Dusty, warm to the touch, it's like stepping
into a luke puddle in August.
That is my fruit. Your fruit is singing
out of its stony core a song
from an opera written twenty years
from now. Then you'll know.

3.
It's like I can't see the dahlias
because I don't have the passcode.
It's like maize, that yellow between
canary and cow hide, is extinct.
We are taking up the telephone poles
because cars keep crashing into them.
The lady on an unswept porch is trying
to smoke a cigarette. A pilot is trying
to fly a plane. A nurse is trying to be
a gardener. I am trying not to find you.

Poor Amy. Poor, poor Amy,
ruining my vacation like that.
But her vacation will get better
from here sun will start shining
in her belly again and my belly
will fill with the furry darkness
of tarantulas. There is a thing
about tarantulas that I know.
They find a corner of a shadow
and they stay there all
weekend. I am standing
in a vacation with my curtains
open to the bouldering mountains.
Shit. The vacation has left. So I am
just standing in a plain old room
looking at a plain old mountain.
A vast plane of birdsong
nearly scalps my pretty head.

I WAS DRUNK ON THE BEACH IN OAXACA

*It was dawn. The darkness was still glued to the
horizon by a squeeze of light. Cruise ships lifted anchors
and curved out of sight. My eyes would not close. They
were like the all-night liquor store on the corner of
Steiner and Hyde.*

Steiner? In Oaxaca?

*Yes, Oaxaca. I was open all night. My heart slid open
and closed like a freezer full of popsicles.*

I'm sorry. Are we talking about the same town? Oaxaca
for lovers?

Oaxaca for Julie and Jason.

And you were able to get drunk there? Impossible.

*But I was looking east. Sun was coming at me like a
church bus. I was standing by the ocean.*

So, you were drunk on the beach in Oaxaca.

*Yes, I was standing on the beach in Oaxaca, hammered,
when I realized I'd gone and done it again.*

Yes, but did you see the water?

*It was too dark to say, but I sensed its presence. I smelled
the seaweed. I heard the echoing snap of a pelican beak.*

It's 10:07 a.m., but it feels noon.
It's October the nineteenth.
It feels like tomorrow. It feels like spring.
It feels like depression. I am elated
but it feels like a horse-drawn carriage.
I wish this recliner were an airplane seat.
Inside the house feels like outside the window.

Practice dysthymia. Practice blood disease.
Put your feet on the floor.
It feels like bamboo. It is linoleum.
Leave your message.
Leave your message.
Call.

A visible trace of an earlier date in this day
A visible trace of an earlier meal in this pan
A trace of a marriage in this postcard
A trace of loss in this win
A great fall of water, a cataract of whiskers
A downpour of boyfriends
It feels like the 1890's. It is the 1980's.

Brother, Brother, Brother, and Brother:
It's happy hour somewhere
It's happy hour in my song
It feels like morning
It's bedtime somewhere

Get the light. It's lights out somewhere.
Love a leaf first. First, love a grain.

It's 3 p.m. and I miss 1 p.m.
I miss lunch. I feel confident that 4
will get here, and I can't wait for 7,
when stepping into the cold
feels like the moment after I flip
my car into an icy lake and I wade out
pulled by the help of strangers. I am
too young to drive. My mother
is at home in front of the stove.
My brother is drumming pencils
at his desk. My girlfriend is still
at practice.   I miss love.

THE SOUVENIR ROOM

This is where I would put a painted wooden lizard
from Oaxaca, were I to have one.
This is where I would lay the hand-woven rug
to pull its reds and yellows across the hearth,
if I had a hearth.
I would hang hammered tin stars here, here and here,
so that they'd glint in the firelight like the same stars
on the wet streets of Oaxaca.
Perhaps, though, I would not be allowed
to bring them on the plane,
due to their sharp edges,
but perhaps I will not have a fire, even,
for you have to go to Oaxaca to get that, too.
Black pottery on this shelf makes a statement:
I have been to Oaxaca,
and I have purchased a tradition.
The spaces on the shelf in the shapes
of jugs and lanterns say something, too.
They say, we are hungry for Oaxaca,
so hungry that to go there would never fill us up.
Perhaps, I don't have the shelf, yet,
for that, too, is in Oaxaca,
along with this room itself,
which is just too big for me to imagine.

THE AMERICANS

The slippery way of arriving is in one's own departure.
A scramble of cold and gin. Americans want the door

back open. The curtain should not have lingered over
glazed, black-walnut New York. The girdle of gray seas

tapers the nation. We are cinched in and ready
to belt out the new anthem. In America, we have

20 ways to sing, *Like, I could care*. They all sound
faintly like, *I could care*. The way *olive juice*

may be mistaken for *I love you*. Olive juice is dirty,
and so is care. I want to be filthy and salty and spilled

all over the floors of elementary school cafeterias.
We don't want to be this kind of woman, hunched

over our desks, snarling. We are flammable
but too big to burn, a wooden planet. We hear

our chandeliers dropping, but they smashed down
generations ago. I'm not talking to you.

I'm talking to me, stooped over my own desk
on which I see a leaf push through black dirt.

A crop, I think. *A bud!* The smallest sprout shows
there is really no America. I still can't stand up.

IF OAXACA MEANS THIS YEAR

Oaxaca there will be a new kind of grass in your front yard
that stays green through the winter and yellows in June.
You will remember how last year you thought about Oaxaca.
And four years ago you thought about four years ahead.
You were right about your son. Think about Oaxaca.
Think about somebody else's Oaxaca. How in January,
he will drive west. Any west. He'll outgrow his fear of wind.
Shave. Now, think of Oaxaca for me. That the people I love
don't die. No, just my son. My son and my husband, at least.
Not my parents. Not Jim. The people I knew in high school.
This could take all of Oaxaca to finish. That Oaxaca moves
in slow motion. Or, we can see Oaxaca like a photograph
of everyone alive on a blanket at the beach. That everyone
feels the flash of the camera in their hearts. That the camera
is really a television, and we feel it looking in on us.
That it feels like the love of a stranger
and everyone watching their televisions can feel it.
That Oaxaca, you don't even need a television to feel it.

Acknowledgments

I want to thank the editors of the following journals who first published parts of this book, often in earlier versions: *27 rue de fleures, 42 Opus, American Poetry Review, BFF Press, Left Facing Bird, Lungfull, The National Poetry Review, The Nervous Breakdown, Tool: A Magazine, Two Serious Ladies, White Whale Review, Zoland Poetry*

The poem "Etiquettes" borrows language from Thich Nhat Hanh's *Peace is Every Step: The Path of Mindfulness in Everyday Life.*

Thank you, C.J., for selecting and editing this manuscript.

For their love and attention, I want to thank the Hugheys, Brantleys, Barrys, Smyths, Johnsons, Daths and Campbells. Most especially, thank you, Chip.

Also from The National Poetry Review Press:

Lucktown by Bryan Penberthy

Bill's Formal Complaint by Dan Kaplan

Gilgamesh at the Bellagio by Karl Elder

Legend of the Recent Past by James Haug

Urchin to Follow by Dorine Jennette

The Kissing Party by Sarah E. Barber

Deepening Groove by Ravi Shankar

The City from Nome by James Grinwis

Fort Gorgeous by Angela Vogel

Able, Baker, Charlie by John Mann

The Wanted by Michael Tyrell

Please visit our website for more information:

www.nationalpoetryreview.com

www.ingramcontent.com/pod-product-compliance
Lightning Source LLC
Chambersburg PA
CBHW021511090426
42739CB00007B/558